1 *above* A recruiting Petty Officer describes the life of a sailor to two likely lads. *c*. 1901

2 *overleaf* The Flag Captain of HMS *Majestic* writing a message from the Admiral, which the signal midshipman will communicate to the Fleet, *c*. 1902

Victorian and Edwardian

NAVY

from old photographs

Commentaries by
John Fabb

Introduction by
A. P. McGowan

Head of the Department of Ships and Deputy Keeper
National Maritime Museum
Greenwich

B. T. BATSFORD LTD

LONDON

First published 1976
© commentaries John Fabb 1976
© Introduction A. P. McGowan 1976

ISBN 0 7134 31 22 9

Printed by The Anchor Press, Tiptree, Essex
for the publishers, B. T. Batsford Limited
4 Fitzhardinge Street
London W1H 0AH

CONTENTS

	illustration numbers
Acknowledgments	
Introduction	
Life at Sea	1–43
Work at Sea	44–64
Training	65–76
Campaigns	77–89
The Royal Marines	90–105
Leisure	106–119
The Royal Navy	120–133
Personalities	134–145
Uniforms	146–172

3 New recruits onboard HMS *Northumberland*, 1901. These men were to be trained as stokers

INTRODUCTION
The Royal Navy 1814–1914

The century between the end of the Napoleonic Wars and the beginning of the First World War saw greater and more widespread changes than any period before or since, notwithstanding the fact that today, while still submerged, a submarine can deliver a devastating blow to a city several hundred miles away. Both the ships and guns of 1814 would have been readily accepted and understood by a seaman of Henry VIII's reign, in say 1547, the year that naval administration was first put on a formal basis. A sailor of 1814, or even 1838, the year of Queen Victoria's coronation, would have been utterly lost had he by some miracle of reincarnation, found himself aboard Admiral Jellicoe's flagship *Iron Duke* in 1914.

After having been almost static for 300 years, everything in the sailor's world changed during a century dominated by industrial technology. Between 1514 and 1814 the one momentous change was wrought by the ability to calculate longitude, as a result of Harrison's work on marine chronometers. Between 1814 and 1914, about the only things that did not change were the timeless sea and sky.

Of all the great developments, the most important was the introduction of the steam engine, which overcame the other great element in the seaman's life: the winds, on which he had hitherto been totally dependent. Following the commercial success of steam early in the century, the Royal Navy ordered its first steam vessel in 1822. Nine years later the first steam fighting ships were ordered. By 1840, Admiral Sir T. Byam Martin, a former Comptroller of the Navy, could comment:

> The fleet which is attended by the greatest number of heavy, well commanded steamers will have an immense advantage. Steamers, if judiciously conducted, will have the power to inflict merciless wounds with impunity.

The Royal Navy's first steam warships were all paddle sloops and frigates, over 60 of which were laid down during the two decades before 1850. However, paddle warships suffered certain disadvantages. Not only did the paddles seriously reduce the space for mounting guns, but they were also dangerously exposed to enemy fire.

The dilemma was resolved during the eighteen-forties when after much argument about the respective merits of the paddle and the screw propeller, the latter was conclusively proved superior. After 1850 paddles were confined to craft for special service, such as tugs and certain river gunboats.

Although the Admiralty adopted the screw propeller, in all but harbour vessels steam was still only an auxiliary means of motive power and was to remain so for another twenty years, until the commissioning of the *Devastation*, 1871, the first major warship designed without sails.

Meanwhile the general appearance of warships changed little during the first half of the century. As late as 1860 HMS *Howe*, 121 guns, was launched, built of wood, a First Rate strictly in the sense that Lord Nelson understood the term, although she had engines as auxiliary power. In the eighteen-forties, experiments had been carried out on the use of iron hulls, but the poor quality of the iron available at that time caused Their Lordships to decide that its tendency to splinter made it unsuitable for warships.

In fact wood was widely used for smaller vessels such as sloops and gunboats until the 'eighties when the mass production of steel made all other materials for warship building obsolete.

At the end of the Napoleonic Wars, the 32-pounder solid round shot was still standard in the Royal Navy. The small explosive payload and the unreliability of the fuse discouraged the use of the other spherical projectiles, known, because of their hollow form, as shells. By 1837, however, the French had developed shells to the stage where guns designed for solid shot could fire shells of a larger calibre which could demonstrably inflict more damage to an opposing warship. The Royal Navy quickly adopted the shell gun as part of its main armament, whilst also developing the weight of both guns and shot in the traditional form. The use of the shell was to have other far-reaching effects on the Royal Navy.

The Crimean War demonstrated the value of iron armour plating and the launching of the French *La Gloire* in 1859 caused considerable concern.

Properly handled, this one ship, a fast frigate built of wood but with a skin of iron armour, could have inflicted severe damage to a large number of ships of the line in the British fleet. When public opinion demanded a counter-measure, the Admiralty responded with HMS *Warrior* the following year; described at the time as the first iron-hulled sea-going armoured ship, and the largest and most powerful warship afloat.

The change to the use of iron and later steel favoured Great Britain more than any other nation at that time since in Britain heavy industry was already well organised and able to expand rapidly.

The success of the improved shell, followed by the equal success of the French armour plating in withstanding it, were the first steps in the battle between guns and armour which were to continue for a hundred years. The next step was the development of the rifled gun and the cylindrical projectile, but in order for the new guns to be effective against the armour available – in addition to her iron hull the *Warrior* had eighteen inches of teak and four and a half inches of iron – the guns had to be so heavy that they caused stability problems for the naval architect.

As a result, for major warships the number of guns was greatly reduced but their arcs of fire were considerably increased by concentrating them in revolving turrets. Thus the *Monarch* of 1868 was the first British ship to mount a gun as large as 12-inch, and of these she had four, each weighing 25 tons, mounted in twin turrets. These guns were all rifled muzzle-loaders, a weapon with which, apart from the short-lived adoption of the unreliable Armstrong breech-loader, the Royal Navy persisted until the mid eighteen-eighties.

Following the invention of the Bessemer process for making steel in bulk, the latter superseded iron as the material for shipbuilding. As a result a reduction of 12–15 per cent was effected in the weight of the hull alone, and even more in the weight of armour. Ships could therefore be built larger with more and heavier guns.

Another factor which made greater size possible was the increased efficiency of the engines. The key to this was the improvement in boiler pressures and in condensers, resulting from the rapidly growing technology. The single cylinder engine of the early days was developed into first the compound and then the triple-expansion engine. With the new type of engine giving a greater range because of the more economical use of coal, sail was finally discarded except for training purposes. The departure of HMS *Temeraire* from the Mediterranean Fleet in 1891 marked the end of sail in the main fleets.

New weapons emerged. The Russians introduced moored mines – then known as torpedoes – during the Crimean War; fifteen years later, largely as a result of the experiments of the Englishman Whitehead, and the Austrian Luppis, the locomotive or 'fish' torpedo as it was first called, was developed. Following the successful ramming tactics of the Austrians against the Italians at the Battle of Lissa in 1864, the ram bow was widely adopted in all the major navies for nearly 40 years. However, the ram, a specially toughened, sharp projection of the bow just below the waterline, never again had the opportunity to achieve the same success in battle, although it claimed several victims as a result of errors when vessels were manoeuvring in close formation. The most notable of these, HMS *Victoria*, sank with the loss of 300 lives including that of the Commander-in-Chief after being struck by the *Camperdown* in 1893.

The introduction of the Whitehead torpedo had far-reaching consequences. It was first seen as the weapon for small but very fast boats designed to make a high speed attack on the main vessels of the enemy fleet. For the first time a single successful blow could sink a capital ship.

The improved engines enabled larger and larger torpedo boats to operate apparently at ever increasing speeds. Torpedo boats capable of accompanying the fleet to sea were followed by the inevitable counter-measure: a torpedo boat not only able to fulfil its original role, but also having a large enough gunnery armament to act as a torpedo boat chaser, or torpedo boat destroyer. By 1914 large ocean-going types had been introduced, capable of keeping the seas with the battle fleet in all weathers; their function had not changed although their name had: they were now simply known as destroyers.

In the 'seventies the tendency had been towards the main units of the fleet having big guns only. The advent of the torpedo boat demanded smaller guns which could be more rapidly trained, fired and reloaded. This requirement led to modifications in guns and ammunition up to six-inch, and also to the development of the belt or magazine-fed guns of the Gatling and Maxim type which, using fixed ammunition, could direct a stream of one-inch bullets at the target.

Important though the torpedo was as a weapon used by fast surface craft, its characteristics suited undersea warfare perfectly, and it found its true vehicle in the submarine which was in service by 1900.

The last decades before World War I also saw further changes. The momentous public appearance of the first steam turbine vessel, the *Turbinia*, at the Diamond Jubilee Review in 1897 heralded a new stage in ship propulsion; within two years the Royal Navy had its first turbine driven warship. Early in the twentieth century, oil fuel was also introduced, although at first it was sprayed on coal.

It was at this point that the Royal Navy produced the warship which left the world breathless and which dondemned all her predecessors to immediate obsolescence:

HMS *Dreadnought*, 1906. Fast (turbine driven), heavily armed with ten 12-inch guns, and as heavily armoured, she alone would have been more than a match for any other pair of warships afloat at that time.

Other navies copied the *Dreadnought* of course, but by 1911 an improved design appeared: the super-dreadnought, armed with 13.5-inch guns of which the *Iron Duke* was one.

Two other innovations of note occurred between the launching of the *Dreadnought* and the outbreak of war: the introduction of radio and the Royal Navy's first use of the aeroplane.

The use of flags for signalling dates from the beginning of the eighteenth century. The semaphore was introduced early in the nineteenth century chiefly for use in harbour and between ships in close company. A combination of the invention of the morse code and the generation of electricity produced the signal lamp, in use in the navy just before 1900. The invention of the wireless transmitter completely revolutionised communications, permitting the latest intelligence to be passed immediately to the Flag Officer or individual captain at sea.

Of the aeroplane in the period before World War I little need be said. Although the Navy was the first service to have its own air arm – the Royal Naval Air Service – its use of aircraft was still in the experimental stage before 1914.

So much for the ships, weapons, and equipment of the Royal Navy between 1814 and 1914; but what of the men?

Generally speaking even in the early twentieth century they were probably very much the same sort of men as those who had served at Trafalgar. They were better educated certainly, in that those who could not read and write were now the exception rather than the rule. In the main, however, their problems were very much the same.

Nothing that they had learned as a landsman was of much use to them, except the universal virtue of common sense. Almost every skill the newly joined seaman had to master was peculiar to the sea – and perhaps even to the Royal Navy, whether it was gunnery, rigging, handling a boat or stoking the enormous furnaces in the blistering heat of the stokehold of a pitching, heaving battleship.

In his dress, although now a uniform, introduced for the lower deck in 1857, the seaman was not so very different from his predecessors who fought with Nelson and Collingwood. Loose trousers, a blouse with a broad square collar, a straw hat and a kerchief – the essential ingredients were still the same. In summer, the uniform was of white canvas duck with a sennet hat; in winter, blue serge and sennet hat. For much of the time, particularly on wooden decks, and especially in the tropics, he would be barefoot. He slept in a hammock slung on a crowded messdeck where he also had his meals and relaxed when he had the opportunity. At sea his favourite relaxation was almost certainly sleeping. Once ashore, if it was not his home port where he might have family ties, his first intent was to enjoy himself with his shipmates, his last to get back on board before his leave was up and then, most probably without a penny of the pay he had drawn.

He was certainly healthier than his forebears, for better qualified doctors and dentists certified that he was fit and unrelenting Gunnery Instructors and Physical Training Instructors did their best to keep him so. Towards the end of the nineteenth century at least, the food was almost certainly better than it had been sixty years earlier. Discipline, although it could still be harsh, was no longer enforced with the threat of the lash. Flogging, although to this day a punishment listed in the Naval Discipline Act, was suspended after 1880.

The modern idea of a fixed engagement carrying a pension came in 1853 with the

Continuous Service Scheme. By this a man served for ten years qualifying for a pension at the end of that time.

For the many minor conflicts in which Britain was involved during the nineteenth century, the sailor was the general handyman. Almost invariably the action required could be dealt with by the nearest unit of the Royal Navy. There was rarely the time or the need to organise an army expeditionary force; in consequence, the British sailor, ably backed up the Royal Marine, Kipling's 'soldier an' sailor too', was asked to do everything but fight a major fleet action, and with the self-reliance of the seaman, did it all extremely well. Bombardment from the sea, suppressing piracy and the Slave Trade, serving far inland in the Naval Brigades of the Indian Mutiny and the South African War, bringing relief at the scene of natural disasters – the navy, it was felt, could do anything.

The officers were probably rather more different from their predecessors of Nelson's day. From the middle of the nineteenth century, formal training before receiving a commission became obligatory. Thereafter junior officers were not only better prepared for the practical training they were to receive, but also they were bound together indefinably by their all having passed through *Britannia* at Portland or later at Dartmouth.

The era was also one which produced personalities, some names such as Keppel and Fremantle recurring time and again; others, such as Beresford and Fisher were new, but all were household names in their time. .

Long periods of peace are no better for officers than men in the Service, and there is no doubt that for many, including very senior officers, the term efficient became synonymous with a spotless perfection that even led to a refusal to permit guns to be fired in practice because the resultant heat blistered the paintwork.

Nevertheless, the policing duties required by scattered colonies undoubtedly gave many officers invaluable experience in independent command. The establishment of the Royal Naval College at Greenwich and of training establishments such as the Gunnery School at Whale Island helped to maintain the professional standards engendered by such officers as Percy Scott and A. K. Wilson. There is little doubt that the twenty years of naval rivalry with Germany did much to whet the keenness to be ready when the day came. As a consequence, notwithstanding the fact that there had been no major naval war for a hundred years, when war was declared on 4 August 1914, the officers and men of the Royal Navy were better prepared for the struggle than had been the case at the start of that first global conflict in 1789.

All this is mirrored in the excellent selection of photographs collected by Mr Fabb. Although sail was rapidly disappearing from the fleet by the time the camera came into popular use, photographs taken aboard the boys' training ships give something of the flavour. The passing of sail however, brought a new torment: coaling ship. No second best for the photographer in this case, but it is still doubtful if the picture can convey the apalling dust which in six hours of coaling reached everywhere. Jack at work and play, undergoing training or medical examination, all these aspects of life in the 'Queen's Navee' or roughly that period are well represented.

The camera produces an excellent record of uniforms and occasionally variations; the dress of the petty officers in the years just before a regulation uniform was introduced; the Admiral who insisted on wearing a top-hat contrary to Queen's Regulations and Admiralty Instructions. However, few people argue with Admirals. . . .

Inevitably, in the early years of the camera, most of the photographs were posed, even those showing action; but this detracts surprisingly little from either the interest or the charm. Inevitably too, in such a collection, many of the photographs are familiar, but mixed with them are several less well-known and a few that are quite new to the public at large.

Of these, some are important historical documents in themselves, as for example that of the three petty officers in 1854, which contains priceless information on the dress worn in the years before uniform was introduced.

The whole makes a pleasing and not inaccurate account of life in the navy in the days when income tax was negligible and 20 shillings could still buy a pound's worth of anything.

ACKNOWLEDGMENTS

The Publisher and Author would like to thank the Earl Mountbatten of Burma, KG, DSO, FRS for his generous encouragement and advice during the preparation of this book. They would also like to thank the following for providing photographs:
By Gracious Permission of Her Majesty the Queen (15, 24, 77, 90, 91, 97, 99, 116, 120, 122–29, 131, 142, 143, 157
Caernarvonshire Record Office (121)
Chatham Public Library (105)
Mansell Collection (81)
National Maritime Museum, Greenwich (22, 30, 32, 53, 82, 110, 112, 119, 134–38, 141, 146–56)
Paul Popper Ltd (130)
Portsmouth Public Library (18, 28, 36, 41, 42, 55, 75, 106, 109, 113, 115, 144, 145, 171)
Royal Marines' Museum, Eastney (98, 102, 104)
Royal Naval Museum, Portsmouth (44, 61, 62, 172)
43 and 133 are from the Publisher's archive and the remainder from the Author's collection.

LIFE AT SEA

4 Laundry day on board, 1902

5   Issuing tobacco and soap rations. The stars on the Petty Officer's sleeve denotes the supply branch. *c*. 1890

6   A boy seaman purchasing bread and ginger beer onboard HMS *Good Hope*. 1901

7 The Flagship transmitting orders to the cruisers of the Fleet by semaphore during the Atlantic manoeuvres of 1903

8 A midshipman ADC ready
to carry orders in port. 1890

9 Captain Churchill of HMS *Nile* coming aboard at Malta. Standing by are the Lieutenant of the Watch with a midshipman and the boatswain's mate, 1898

10 *top* A cadet on board HMS *Britannia* writes home to mother, 1898

11 *above* Two sailors at the wheel of HMS *Calliope, c.* 1895

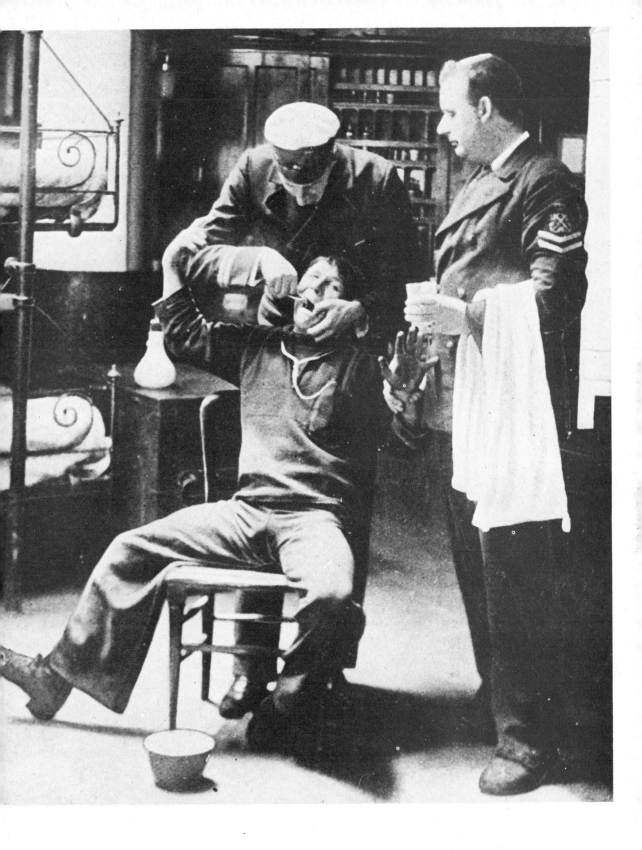

12   Dentistry on board HMS *Powerful* in the 1890s

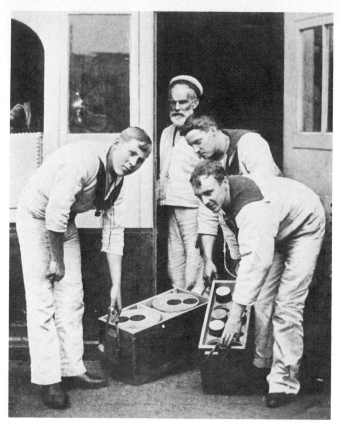

13   Issuing gun cotton, 1890. Cotton mixed with concentrated nitric acid retains the appearance of ordinary cotton waste; it does not explode except in a confined space

14   A gun crew at work on HMS *Calliope*, 1898

15   The upper deck of HMS *Serapis* on the royal tour of 1875

16   Serving out the fresh meat ration in HMS *Talbot*, 1896. 1 lb of meat was issued to each man every day in port; at sea the ration was 1 lb of salt pork on every other day, and on alternate days either 1 lb of salt beef or $\frac{3}{4}$ lb of preserved meats

17 Cooks and stewards on board a battleship in the Mediterranean, 1896. Maltese were often employed aboard ships of the Mediterranean Fleet

18 Dinner time on the lower deck, *c.* 1890

19 The captain and his officers at dinner aboard HMS *Sans Pareil*, 1899. A Royal Marine officer can be seen sitting on the right

20   Royal Navy and Royal Marine officers playing whist after dinner, *c.* 1890

21   *opposite* Rum was issued at six bells in the forenoon watch. *c.* 1898

22   Members of the crew at leisure in HMS *Coquete*, 1855. Note the pet monkeys at the front

23   HRH The Prince of Wales's barge and crew in tropical kit during the royal tour of India in 1875

24   *overleaf* HMS *Calliope* hoisting sail, *c.* 1895

25 Reporting a signal to the officer of the watch aboard HMS *Diadem,* a 1st Class Cruiser, Captain W. H. Graham. 1898

26 *opposite top* Kit inspection on board HMS *Ganges* in 1890. One of the last ships of the line in commission, *Ganges* was paid off in 1861 and became a training ship for boys at Falmouth

27 *opposite bottom* The wardroom of a warship *c.* 1890. On larger ships some degree of comfort could be achieved by way of carpets and easy chairs

28 The admiral's cabin in HMS *Trafalgar*. The degree of comfort depended upon the officer's purse

29 Pay day on board HMS *Royal Sovereign*, 1875. The paymaster hands the money to the sailor who puts it on the top of his cap. The master-at-arms at the rear checks the men's names

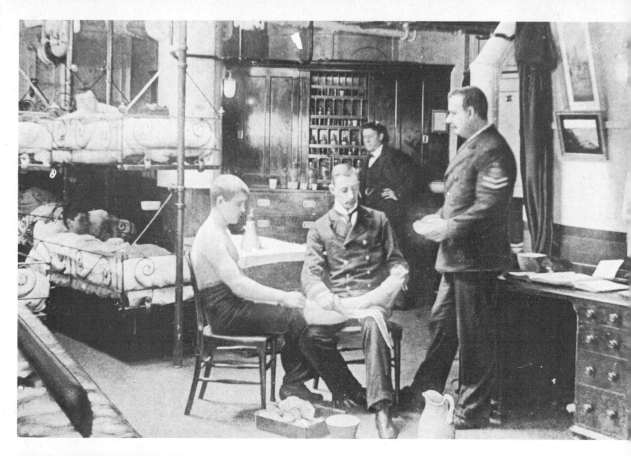

30 *above* The sick berth on board the cruiser HMS *Powerful, c.* 1898

31 *left* Two recruits await with trepidation the verdict of this petty officer, *c.* 1910

32 *opposite top* Royal Navy officers and their ladies on board a warship, 1869. A rear-admiral stands on the right wearing the Order of the Bath on his frock coat

33 *opposite bottom* The band of HMS *Powerful* in 1899. All larger warships were allowed bands

34 *left* Divine service in a warship, *c.* 1890

35 *below* The auction of a dead man's effects by the master-at-arms, *c.* 1890. The prices were run up to a generous figure for the benefit of the widow

36 *opposite* Landing the Duke of Connaught's elephant at Portsmouth in 1908, to the amusement of the sailors

37   A stretcher-party carrying a wounded man to the hospital base during manoeuvres in Malta, 1903

38   *opposite top* A sister of Queen Alexandra's Royal Naval Nursing Service receiving a wounded sailor at Malta during manoeuvres, 1905

39   *opposite bottom* New recruits being received on board for sea-service, 1899

40 A sailor up to see the medical officer, 1910

41 The end of HMS *Victoria* after her collision with the *Camperdown* on 22 June 1893 in which 300 lives were lost, including that of the commander-in-chief

42 The victims of an explosion on board HMS *Comet* in 1904 were given a naval funeral with full honours. The gun-carriages bearing the coffins are drawn by the ship's company

43 A sailor home from the sea in 1908, telling a young lad an unlikely story

WORK AT SEA

44 *below* Stokers at work in the battleship HMS *Majestic, c.* 1910

45 *opposite* In the engine room of a battle cruiser, *c.* 1910

46 *opposite* Relaying bricks
over a firebox in the stokehold
of HMS *Nelson*, 1910

47 *above* Stokers being trained
aboard HMS *Nelson* in 1910

48 Dhobeying hanging out to dry aboard HMS *St Vincent,* 1908. In the Royal Navy all washing is dhobeying, a term corrupted from the Hindustani dhobi, perhaps a relic from the naval brigade which served in the Indian Mutiny

49 Reefing topsails in the training ship HMS *Impregnable,* 1896

50 *opposite top* Repairing sails in a warship, *c.* 1890. Some vessels still had auxiliary sails in the later years of Queen Victoria's reign

51 *opposite bottom* Training the crew to weigh the anchor in an emergency by means of a manual capstan, a task unaltered since the days of Nelson

52 *above* Coaling a warship, *c.*1910, the worst and dirtiest job on board. All hands took part, including the officers, and all parts of the ship became covered in a fine coal dust

53 *left* Damaged yards being replaced at Malta in 1899, a difficult task amid the mass of rigging

54 *above* Rescuing ship's documents from the capsized HMS *Gladiator*, 2nd Class Cruiser, off the Isle of Wight, 1908

55 *overleaf* Hands 'walking away with it' while the band gives some encouragement

56   Painting ship, 1908

57   Royal Navy divers, 1896.
These men were trained at the
submarine classes at Portsmouth,
Devonport and Sheerness

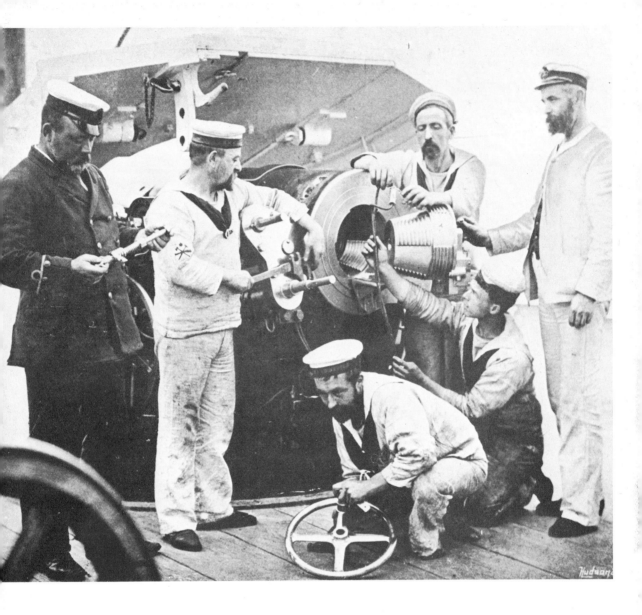

58 Repairing one of the six-inch guns aboard the battleship HMS *Edinburgh, c.* 1898

61   *below* Repairing and
cleaning ship's lamps, 1910

59   *above* Furling and stowing
headsails, 1903

60   *left* Scraping the deck of a
warship, *c.* 1895. The ship's
mascot looks on

62 Scrubbing the decks. On the right can be seen the signal lockers, 1911

63   Sewing flags for the Fleet in the workshops at HM Dockyard, Chatham, 1902

64   Women spinning hemp for cables at HM Dockyard, Chatham, 1902

TRAINING

65 Physical drill at Portsmouth, 1890. The might of the Victorian Navy can be seen in the background

66 *right* Teaching a boy seaman to swim, 1910

67 *below* A class of midshipmen in the cruiser HMS *Blake* receiving instruction on the sextant, 1895

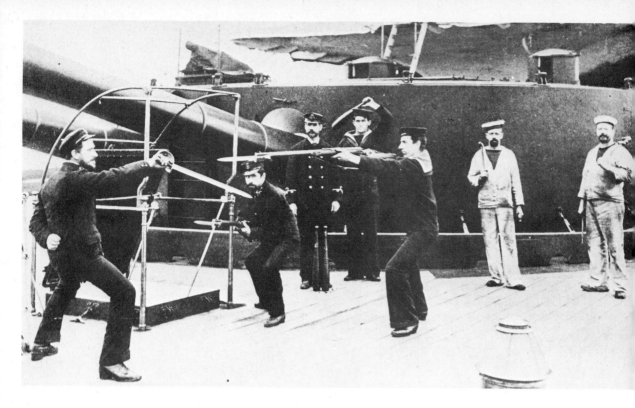

68 Cutlass versus bayonet, 1897

69 Boys being taught to box the compass, 1902

70 Seamen being instructed in knots, bends and hitches, 1899

71 A naval square prepares to receive cavalry during training at Whale Island, Portsmouth, in 1896. Because of the many punitive expeditions carried out by the Royal Navy it was necessary that these military manoeuvres should be learnt

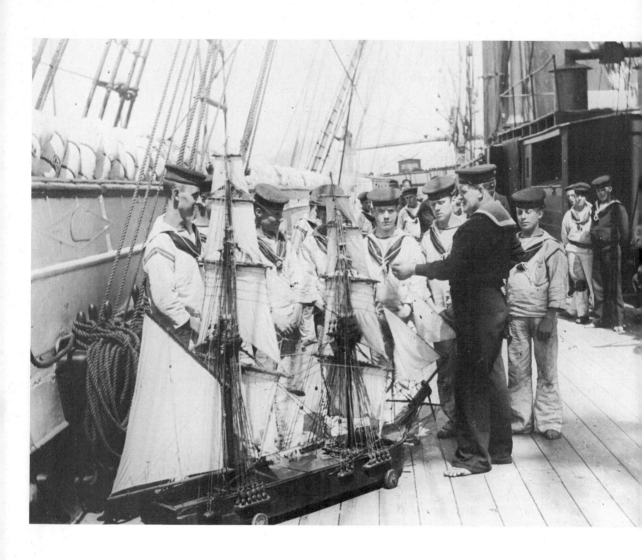

72   Teaching boys the rigging and sails, 1910

73 Instructors from HMS *Excellent* demonstrating with a Maxim machine gun mounted on wheels for use with a landing party, 1896

74 *opposite top* Midshipmen at lessons in the cruiser HMS *Theseus*, 1896. After passing-out at the end of a two-year course they served at sea for four years and were then ready for the examinations for a lieutenant's commission

75 *opposite bottom* Sailors at Whale Island landing a gun and limber from a small boat. The men are wearing white uniforms with gaiters, *c.* 1900

76 *above* After signalmen had learnt each signal flag they then practiced the use of their knowledge on the Tufnell model. Devonport, 1898

CAMPAIGNS

77 *below* Three sailors of the Crimea War, 1854. From the left, Charles Brooks, Admiral's Coxswain, HMS *Britannia*; John Stanley, Boatswain, HMS *Sampson*; and Edward Penelly, Leading Seaman, HMS *Sans Pareil*

78 *opposite top* Officers on the quarterdeck of the wooden screw frigate HMS *Shannon* in 1857. Captain William Peel, standing on the right, led his crew with the ships guns in the relief of Lucknow during the Indian Mutiny

79 *opposite bottom* Captain Roderick Dew and his officers in the screw corvette HMS *Encounter*. This ship was in action during the China War, 1860

80 Sailors examining the Egyptian fortress at Alexandria after the British bombardment in 1882

81 Royal Naval personnel, under Captain Fitzroy, move along the railway during the Egyptian War of 1882. The armoured train mounts a 40-pdr gun and several Gatling machine guns

82 Gardner machine gun crews from HMS *Hecla* which saw action at Suakim and the Bay of Trinkitat, in the Sudan War in 1884

83 Lord Charles Beresford in a sailor's cap with Field Marshal Lord Wolseley. Lord Beresford acted as Port Captain on the Staff of the General Commanding the forces in Egypt in the quest to rescue General Gordon in 1885

84 *above* The town of Mwele after its capture in 1895 by the crew of the cruiser HMS *St George*. The prevention of the Slave Trade in East Africa was a prime task for the Royal Navy

85 Midshipmen from the cruiser HMS *Terrible* waiting to go ashore during the South African War, 1899

86 Officers of the Naval Brigade sent to assist Lord Methuen during the South African War, 1899. All the officers numbered were killed in action

87 *opposite top* The gun crew
working a 12-pdr landed from
the cruiser HMS *Powerful* during
the seige of Ladysmith, 1900

88 *opposite bottom* A group of
sailors from the cruiser HMS
Orlando on their way to Peking
during the Boxer rebellion, 1900

89 *above* The crew of the
training ship HMS *Lion* seen
ready to go ashore as a landing
party in times of strife, complete
with Pioneers and ship's band,
c. 1896

THE ROYAL MARINES

90 Royal Marine band, Portsmouth Division, in Burma during the royal tour of HMS *Serapis* in 1875–6

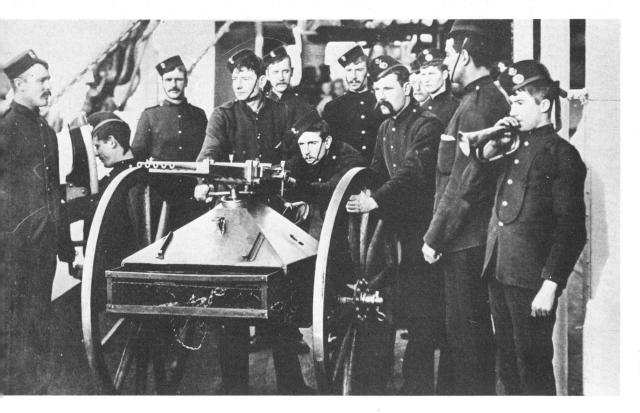

91 A sailor assisting a Royal Marine at an assignation, 1899
92 Royal Marines posing with a Gardner machine gun, 1896. Note the shoulder piece of the quick-firing gun on the left
93 Royal Marine Light Infantry at bayonet exercise on the upper deck of the cruiser HMS *Melampos* at Kingstown, Ireland, in 1897

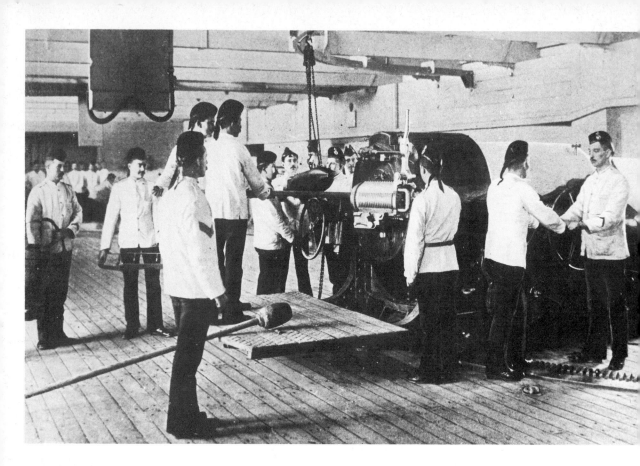

94 *opposite top* Royal Marines handling a 9·2-inch gun capable of piercing 19-inch armour plate, *c.* 1890

95 *opposite bottom* Royal Marines gather round the ample figure of the ship's butcher, *c.* 1898

96 *right* Two Royal Marine artillerymen in 1855: Gunner Samuel Smith, 8th Company and Bombardier William Hewlett, 12th Company

97 *below* A group of Royal Marines at Portsmouth in 1855: Corporal William Chase, Private Charles Fletcher, Private Benjamin Bush, Sgt. Henry Edsell and Private Timothy Lyons

98 Royal Marine family group, 1861

99 Captain Edmund Brighouse
Snow, Royal Marine Light
Infantry, c. 1868

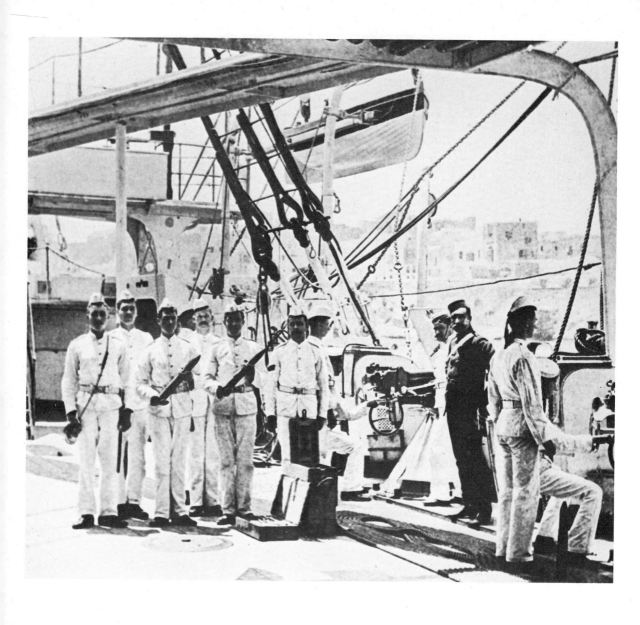

100 Royal Marines manning a 6-pdr quick-firing gun on board the battleship HMS *Camperdown* in 1896

101 *right* A group of Royal Marines and members of the Rifle Brigade who received the Crimea medals from HM Queen Victoria on 18 May 1855

102 *below* The Royal Marines on parade at their new barracks at Eastney, Portsmouth, *c.* 1870

103 No soldier in uniform was allowed to encircle a young lady's waist with his arm. No such order existed in the Royal Navy. *c.* 1899

104 Royal Marine cyclists at Eastney barracks Portsmouth, *c.* 1890. The officer is mounted on a tricycle

105 The Royal Marine band leaving the barracks at Chatham, *c.* 1890

LEISURE

106 *left* One of the barrack rooms at Whale Island, Portsmouth, *c.* 1890. Note the crockery neatly placed on the right-hand wall

107 *above* Jack out with a nursemaid, *c.* 1900

108   The mandoline band of the cruiser HMS *Arethusa* while in the Mediterranean in 1895

109 *above* Visitors on board
the flagship during the naval
review of August 1902

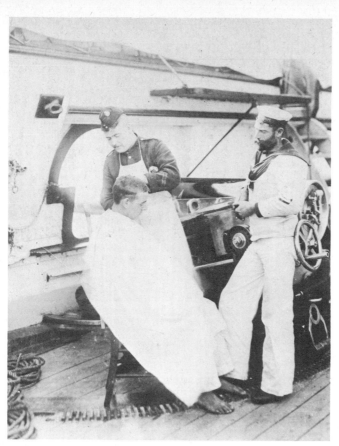

110 *left* A Royal Marine cutting a sailor's hair aboard the screw corvette HMS *Calliope*, 1890

111 *below* Ships company on shore leave at Las Palmas, 1900. Note the topical names given to the donkeys

112 *right* Sailors at Portsmouth arriving for shore leave, *c.* 1890

113 *below* Sailors buying postcards at a French port, *c.* 1900

114 *opposite* 'Jolly Jack on the Town', 1899

115 *above* Sailors on a roundabout at a fair in Brest, *c.* 1900

116 The cast of HMS *Pinafore* at the new *Britannia* Royal Naval College, Dartmouth, *c.* 1910. The late
Duke of Windsor can be seen in the back row, second from right

117 *left* Home on leave, *c.* 1890.
Note the dress fashion popular
for both girls and boys at this
period

118 *below* Sailors dancing

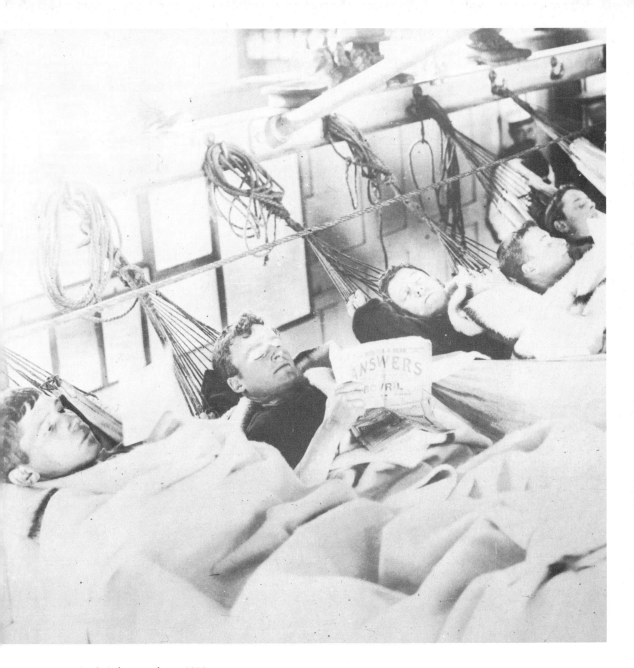

119 At rest in their hammocks. *c.* 1890

THE ROYAL NAVY

120   *below* The Prince of Wales (left) and Prince Alfred, Duke of Edinburgh, 20 August 1853

121   *opposite* Queen Victoria coming ashore from the royal yacht at Holyhead, *c.* 1875

122 *opposite* Prince Louis of
Battenburg in ball dress 1877.
A naturalised British subject in
1868, he rose to be First Sea
Lord in 1912

123 *above* Prince Alfred, Duke
of Edinburgh, August 1858, in
the uniform of a midshipman

124   *above* The two sons of
The Prince of Wales in 1874:
Albert Victor, Duke of Clarence
and Prince George, late King
George V

125   *right* The Prince of Wales's
children in 1874. Standing:
Princess Louise and Prince
Albert Victor, Duke of Clarence;
seated: left to right, Princess
Maude, Prince George, Princess
Victoria

126 *left* Prince Alfred, Duke of Edinburgh at Sydney, Australia in 1867. The second son of Queen Victoria, he became a Rear-Admiral in 1878 and succeeded as the Duke of Saxe-Coburg-Gotha in 1893

127 *below* Prince George (late King George V) and on the right, Prince Albert Duke of Clarence, learning to splice in HMS *Britannia*

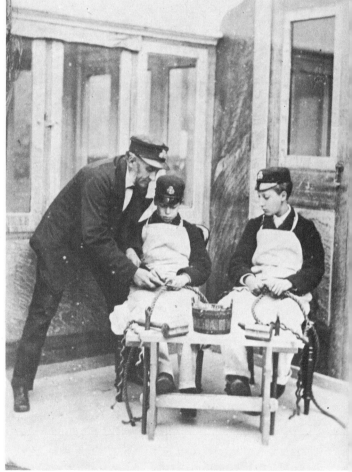

128 Prince Albert Victor, Duke of Clarence, and Prince George, as members of the crew of cutter,
23 July 1878

129 *above* The German William II in the uniform of an Admiral of the Fleet, an honour bestowed by his grandmother, Queen Victoria in 1889

130 *opposite* King Edward VII with the Prince of Wales (later King George V) and his grandsons later King Edward VIII and George VI, *c.* 1905

131 *left* Prince Edward, later King Edward VIII, on board the cruiser HMS *Crescent* in 1898

132 *below* Captain Prince Louis of Battenburg with his family and officers on board the battleship HMS *Implacable* in 1902. On his right, Princess Alice (mother of Prince Philip), on Princess Louis's knee, Prince Louis, (who became Admiral of the Fleet, Earl Mountbatten of Burma), on her left Princess Louise (later Queen of Sweden)

133 Their Majesties King George V and Queen Mary with the Prince of Wales and Princess Mary, landing at Kingstown, Dublin 1911

PERSONALITIES

134 John Roome, *c.* 1850, who claimed to have assisted in the hoisting of Nelson's signal at Trafalgar in 1805

135 *left* Joseph Scudamore,
c. 1850, a survivor of Trafalgar

136 *below* James Sherman,
c. 1850, a survivor of Trafalgar

137 Admiral Sir James Alexander Gordon, *c.* 1849. A 36-pdr ball took his leg off above the knee joint in 1811 when he was serving as Captain of the frigate HMS *Active*, 38-guns. In this action he took the French frigate *La Pomone*

138 Bosun Shepherd VC. In 1854 during the Crimean War he twice proceeded in a punt into Sevastapol Harbour with an explosive to attack Russian ships

139 Rear-Admiral H. J. Raby VC, CB, who served in the Black Sea and landed with a Naval Brigade in the Crimea in 1855 where he won the Victoria Cross for bringing in wounded under severe fire. He later distinguished himself in the suppression of the slave trade

140 *left* Rear-Admiral Charles Davis Lucas VC. While acting mate in HMS *Hecla* during the Crimea War, during the attack on Bomasund, he picked up a live shell which had landed on the deck and threw it overboard

141 *left* Admiral Lord Charles Beresford of Metermmeh and Curraghmore. He served in the Egyptian War of 1882 and in the Sudan War of 1884. An active member of Parliament, he died in 1919

142 *opposite* Admiral The Hon. Sir Henry Keppel (1809–1904). Admiral Keppel was instrumental in putting down piracy off the coast of China and he also commanded a Naval Brigade in the Crimea 1854–56. He was made Admiral of the Fleet in 1877

143 *left* Admiral of the Fleet Lord Fisher, 1841–1920. He entered the Navy in 1854 and fought in the Crimean War and the China War of 1859–60. He commanded MHS *Inflexible* in 1882 and was First Sea Lord from 1904–1910

144 *opposite* The Rt Hon. Winston Churchill, First Lord of the Admiralty, on board the Admiralty yacht HMS *Enchantress* in 1912

146 Commander James Fitzjames in 1845. A member of the Franklin Expedition to the Arctic, he is seen wearing the undress uniform of 1833–56, with epaulettes and peaked cap

UNIFORMS

145 Commander R. F. Scott, *c.* 1908, and some of his officers on the bridge while returning to Portsmouth. He was promoted captain before his expedition to the South Pole in 1910

147 *left* Lieutenant Graham Gore of the discovery ship HMS *Erebus* in 1845. He is wearing the undress uniform which could be worn without epaulettes; note the band of gold lace round the cap

148 *right* 1st Master, 1845. Although masters were allowed the double-breasted jacket of executive officers, this master is wearing the old pattern single-breasted jacket with ten equidistant buttons

149 Bosun Bradshaw, *c.* 1860, wearing a warrant officer's round jacket with brass buttons on the cuffs. By this date the cap badge was in general use

150 Sir Lambert Baynes in 1860, wearing a frock coat with Royal Navy buttons. The top hat does not conform with dress regulations for officers

151 *right* John Reeman of the second rate HMS *London* in 1859 just after her conversion to a screw ship of 72-guns. Note the loose hanging clothes, the long ends of the cap ribbon and the ship's name without letters HMS

152 *below* A group of officers by a smooth-bore muzzle loader, *c.* 1860. The peaked cap, introduced in 1856, complete with anchor wreath and crown cap badge was also worn by warrant officers

153 *left* Assistant Paymaster, 1863. This rank was introduced in 1842; note the epaulettes without bullion fringes and the single-breated tail coat

154 *above* Naval aide-de-camp to the queen, *c.* 1864. This appointment was distinguished by the gold and scarlet shoulder sash, which was abolished in 1874 and replaced by the aiguillettes

155   Admiral Sir Phipps
Hornby in 1867 wearing the
full dress uniform for flag
officers 1856–91; note the
irregular manner of wearing
decorations

156 *left* Sub-Lieutenant 1879 in the frock coat of the pattern worn 1863–91; the peaked cap of the period also can be clearly seen

157 *left* Commander Frederick G. D. Bedford, of MHS *Serapis* in 1876, wearing full dress uniform with the white helmet worn in the tropics. The puggaree is blue; the spike was removed in 1891. White uniform was not introduced until 1885

158 *opposite top* Two sailors with Scottish fishermen *c.* 1845. The straw hats were painted black

159 *opposite bottom* A group of cadets aboard HMS *Britannia* in 1880. Note the small caps and double-breasted jackets which were their uniform at this time; the lanyards and cuff stripes denote cadet captains

160   A petty officer on board the royal yacht *Victoria and Albert*

161 Picquet duty officers from the battleship HMS *Nile* in 1890: a lieutenant RN and a Royal Marine officer wearing the white tropical uniform

162 *left* Officers' full dress 1891–1901. Officers from the cruiser HMS *Theseus* in 1896: Captain Charles Campbell CB, with Commander R. Bacon and Commander S. Corden

163 *right* Sailors' No. 1 dress in 'Whites' *c.* 1896: white duck with sennet hat

164 *left* Charles Annear the master-at-arms of the training ship HMS *Lion* in 1897. The N and P on each side of the crown on the collar badges stand for naval police. The master-at-arms is the only man on the lower deck entitled to wear an officers' sword

166 *below* A seaman from HMS *Excellent* (gunnery training) equipped for a landing party *c.* 1898

167 Petty officers from the battleship HMS *Magnificent* in number one dress in 1908, with a PO 1st Class on the right. Frocks tucked into the tops of the trousers were abolished in 1906 and the sennet hat disappeared in 1921

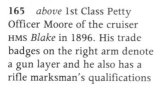

165 *above* 1st Class Petty Officer Moore of the cruiser HMS *Blake* in 1896. His trade badges on the right arm denote a gun layer and he also has a rifle marksman's qualifications

168 *right* A Krooman from the Ascension Island in 1908, at that time under control of the Admiralty. The little girl is the daughter of Brigadier General F. W. Lumsden VC, CB, DSO and three bars, of the Royal Marines

169 *left* A Sub-Lieutenant in ball dress, 1891–1903

170 *opposite* 1st Class Petty Officer in landing rig, *c.* 1900; note the cutlass worn on the left hip

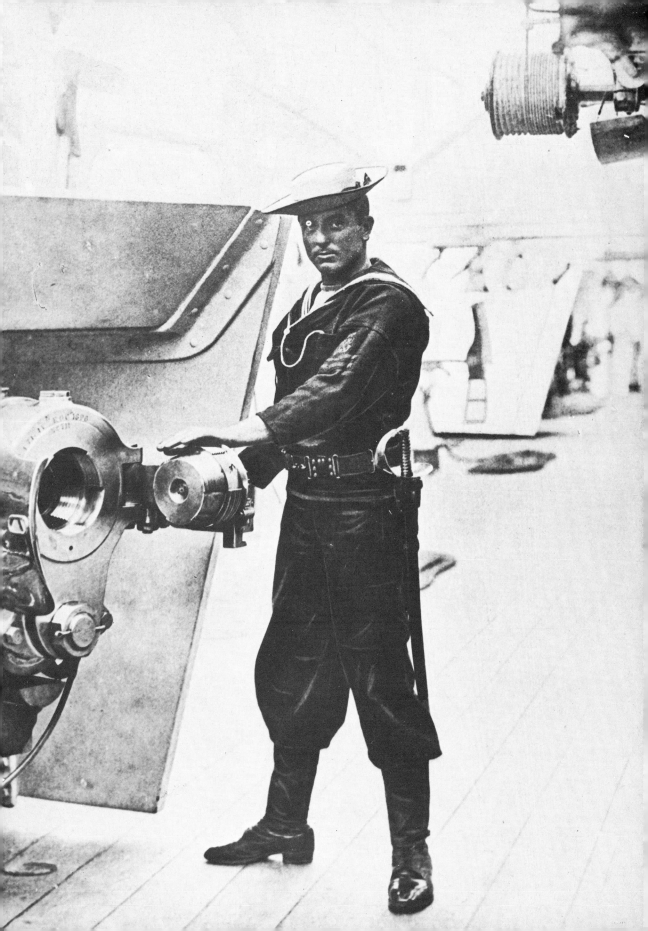

171 A group of officers of the Royal Naval Reserve, *c.* 1910. The cuff lace is the most distinguishing difference from the Royal Navy. The buttons and sword belt clasp carried the letters RNR and the epaulettes and badge consist of an anchor encircled by the words Royal Naval Reserve.

172   Chief Boatswain in full dress *c*. 1900. The tail coat is without epaulettes; the cuff stripe, half an inch wide was introduced in 1865.

photography

F/M — SFB
13101729